Lerner SPORTS

SUPER SPORTS TEAMS

INSIDE THE LAS VEGAS ACES

ANNE E. HILL

Lerner Publications ◆ Minneapolis

Lerner Publications Company
An imprint of Lerner Publishing Group, Inc.
241 First Avenue North
Minneapolis, MN 55401 USA

For reading levels and more information, look up this title at www.lernerbooks.com.

Main body text set in Aptifer Slab LT Pro / Typeface provided by Linotype AG

Library of Congress Cataloging-in-Publication Data

Names: Hill, Anne E., 1974- author.
Title: Inside the Las Vegas Aces / Anne E. Hill.
Description: Minneapolis : Lerner Publications, [2023] | Series: Super sports teams (Lerner sports) | Includes bibliographical references and index. | Audience: Ages 7–11 | Audience: Grades 4–6 | Summary: "The Las Vegas Aces have yet to win a WNBA Championship title, but their future is bright. Explore their beginnings, their record-breaking players, and their mission to become the best in the WNBA"— Provided by publisher.
Identifiers: LCCN 2022013921 (print) | LCCN 2022013922 (ebook) | ISBN 9781728476094 (library binding) | ISBN 9781728478678 (paperback) | ISBN 9781728485188 (ebook)
Subjects: LCSH: Las Vegas Aces (Basketball team)—Juvenile literature. | Women's National Basketball Association—Juvenile literature.
Classification: LCC GV885.52.L37 H55 2023 (print) | LCC GV885.52.L37 (ebook) | DDC 796.32309793/135—dc23/eng/20220603

LC record available at https://lccn.loc.gov/2022013921

TABLE OF CONTENTS

Carolyn Swords (*top left*) wins the ball for the Aces in a playoff game against the Connecticut Sun.

PLAYOFF SUCCESS

FACTS AT A GLANCE

- The team has been called the Starzz, Silver Stars, Stars, and **ACES**.
- **MARGO DYDEK** played for the team for seven years. Dydek was the tallest player in Women's National Basketball Association (WNBA) history.
- The team moved to **LAS VEGAS, NEVADA**, in 2018.
- Head coach **BECKY HAMMON** played on the team for eight seasons.

No one watching the 2020 WNBA Semifinals had expected this. The Las Vegas Aces had lost only four games all season. But in Game 1 of the Semifinals, the Connecticut Sun shocked fans by beating the Aces by 25 points.

Game 2 was a back-and-forth battle with the Aces winning 83–75. The win was thanks to star forward A'ja Wilson. She scored 29 points and grabbed seven rebounds for Las Vegas. The Sun came from behind to win Game 3. Then the Aces won Game 4. The series was tied 2–2.

The 2020 WNBA Playoffs took place as COVID-19 spread around the world. To avoid spreading the disease, no fans were in the stands. All the playoff teams played in the same arena in Bradenton, Florida.

The Aces had beaten the Sun twice during the regular season. Las Vegas entered the playoffs as the top-ranked team. They had finished their season tied with the Seattle Storm for the best record in the league. Las Vegas also had a full week of rest before facing the Sun in the playoffs. But the Sun were playing tough. The series came down to the final game.

Game 5 was a hard battle. The Aces turned up the heat to prove they were the better team. Wilson led Las Vegas with 23 points, 11 rebounds, and four assists. Las Vegas held the Sun to just 18 points in the second half. The Sun had a chance to tie the game in the final seconds, but they couldn't do it. The Aces advanced to the WNBA Finals. The final score was 66–63. It was the second trip to the Finals for Las Vegas. They would face the Storm for the WNBA Championship.

A'ja Wilson (*left*) ranked first in the WNBA for blocks in 2020.

The Aces celebrate their amazing Game 5 win over the Connecticut Sun during the 2020 WNBA Playoffs.

Margo Dydek was seventh in the WNBA for free throws made for two-straight seasons, from 1998 to 1999.

STARZZ TO ACES

The WNBA's first season was in 1997. The Las Vegas Aces were then the Utah Starzz. That year, the Starzz had the worst record in the league. That meant they picked first in the 1998 Draft.

The Starzz chose 7 foot, 2-inch (2.2 m) center Margo Dydek with the first overall pick. She was the tallest player in WNBA history. But the team didn't improve right away. Two years later, the Starzz had a winning season.

Dydek (*center*) stood several inches taller than some of the WNBA's tallest players.

The Starzz went to the playoffs in 2001 and 2002. But they did not advance to the Finals. After the 2002 season, the owner of the San Antonio Spurs bought the Starzz. The Spurs are a National Basketball Association team.

The team moved to San Antonio, Texas, and became the San Antonio Silver Stars. The Silver Stars had losing records in all of their first four seasons. In 2007, the team found new talent in trades and draft picks. The new players helped the Silver Stars become a force in the WNBA.

Becky Hammon (*right*) slips past Tangela Smith of the Phoenix Mercury to score a basket.

ACES FACT

The Aces play at the Mandalay Bay Resort and Casino in Las Vegas. Mark Davis is the team's owner. Davis also owns the National Football League's Las Vegas Raiders.

Vickie Johnson (*second from right*) avoids a block and puts the ball in the net in a game against the Detroit Shock.

In 2008, the Silver Stars went to the WNBA Finals for the first time. They lost to the Detroit Shock. The Silver Stars had several up-and-down seasons following that loss. In 2014, they changed their name to the San Antonio Stars.

The Stars had a terrible 8–26 record in 2017. After the season, the team moved to Las Vegas and became the Las Vegas Aces. Their bad record in 2017 meant they had the first overall draft pick in 2018. They chose Wilson from the University of South Carolina.

Wilson (*right*) has been the Aces' top scorer since she joined the team in 2018.

Wilson proved to be a great player for the Aces. She helped the team improve enough to make the playoffs in 2020 and 2021. The Aces began to thrive in Las Vegas.

On the last day of 2021, the Aces hired Becky Hammon as head coach. She is the highest-paid coach in the WNBA. The former Aces player is the only person to have her number retired by the team. To honor Hammon, no Aces player will ever wear number 25 again.

Before she became the Aces' head coach, Hammon was the first full-time female assistant coach in the National Basketball Association.

Wilson (*left*) won the WNBA's Rookie of the Year award in 2018.

AMAZING MOMENTS

The Aces have made it to the WNBA Playoffs 12 times since their first season in 1997. But in Utah and Texas, they struggled to play well every year. They missed the playoffs in more than half of their seasons in San Antonio.

After moving to Las Vegas in 2018, the Aces were eager to get their first win. On June 1, they faced the Washington Mystics in Las Vegas. The Aces were hot from the start. They scored 25 points in the first quarter. They took the lead and never looked back. Wilson scored 26 points, and Las Vegas won 85–73. It was the team's first of many victories on their new home court.

Kayla McBride (*right*) played seven seasons with the Aces. She helped the team reach the playoffs three times.

The Aces soon became a force in the WNBA. Beginning in 2019, they made it to the playoffs three years in a row. They were getting closer to their goal of winning a championship.

In 2020, the team's hunt for their first WNBA title appeared to be over. The Aces had tied for the league's best regular-season record that year at 18–4. That meant they could skip the first two rounds of the playoffs. Fans were hopeful that Wilson could lead the team to victory.

The Aces defeated the Connecticut Sun to advance to the WNBA Finals. To win the championship, Las Vegas had to beat the Seattle Storm. The Storm were packed with superstar players such as Sue Bird, Jewell Loyd, and Breanna Stewart.

Angel McCoughtry was a star player for 10 seasons with the Atlanta Dream before joining the Aces in 2020.

The teams battled in Game 1 of the Finals. Angel McCoughtry scored 20 points and Wilson had 19 for Las Vegas. But Stewart and Loyd combined for 65 points for Seattle. The Storm won 93–80. The rest of the series didn't go any better for Las Vegas. Seattle won the next two games and the WNBA title.

In 2021, the Aces entered the playoffs with the second-best record in the league at 24–8. Again, they could skip the first two rounds of the playoffs. They faced the Phoenix Mercury in the Semifinals. The Aces had beaten the Mercury twice during the regular season. But in the playoffs, the Aces lost to the Mercury in five games.

ACES FACT

The Aces mascot is a gray-and-white hare named BUCKET$. A hare looks similar to a rabbit. Wearing an Aces jersey, BUCKET$ dances on the court, takes photos with fans, and cheers for the team.

BUCKET$ became the team mascot in 2018 when the Aces moved to Las Vegas.

Hammon (*center*) averaged more than 14 points per game for six of her eight seasons with the Aces despite being just 5 feet, 6 inches (1.7 m) tall.

ACE SUPERSTARS

The Aces owe most of their success to their amazing players. The team's first star was also its tallest. Dydek was the tallest active female basketball player in the world.

Dydek was born in Poland in 1974. In 1998, the Starzz chose her with the number one pick in the WNBA Draft. She played for the team for seven seasons. She is the all-time leader in blocks in the WNBA with 877 in 323 games. Dydek led the league in blocks nine times.

Defenders found it difficult to block Dydek (*right*).

Hammon came to the San Antonio Stars in 2007. Fans and teammates called her Big Shot Becky for her scoring ability. In 2008, she led her team to their first WNBA Finals appearance.

Hammon was one of the WNBA's top-ten scorers four different seasons.

ACES FACT

In 2021, Wilson and Aces teammate Chelsea Gray played for the USA Basketball Women's National Team (USBWNT). They helped win the gold medal at the Olympic Games in Tokyo, Japan. Wilson scored 19 points and Gray had six points in the gold-medal game.

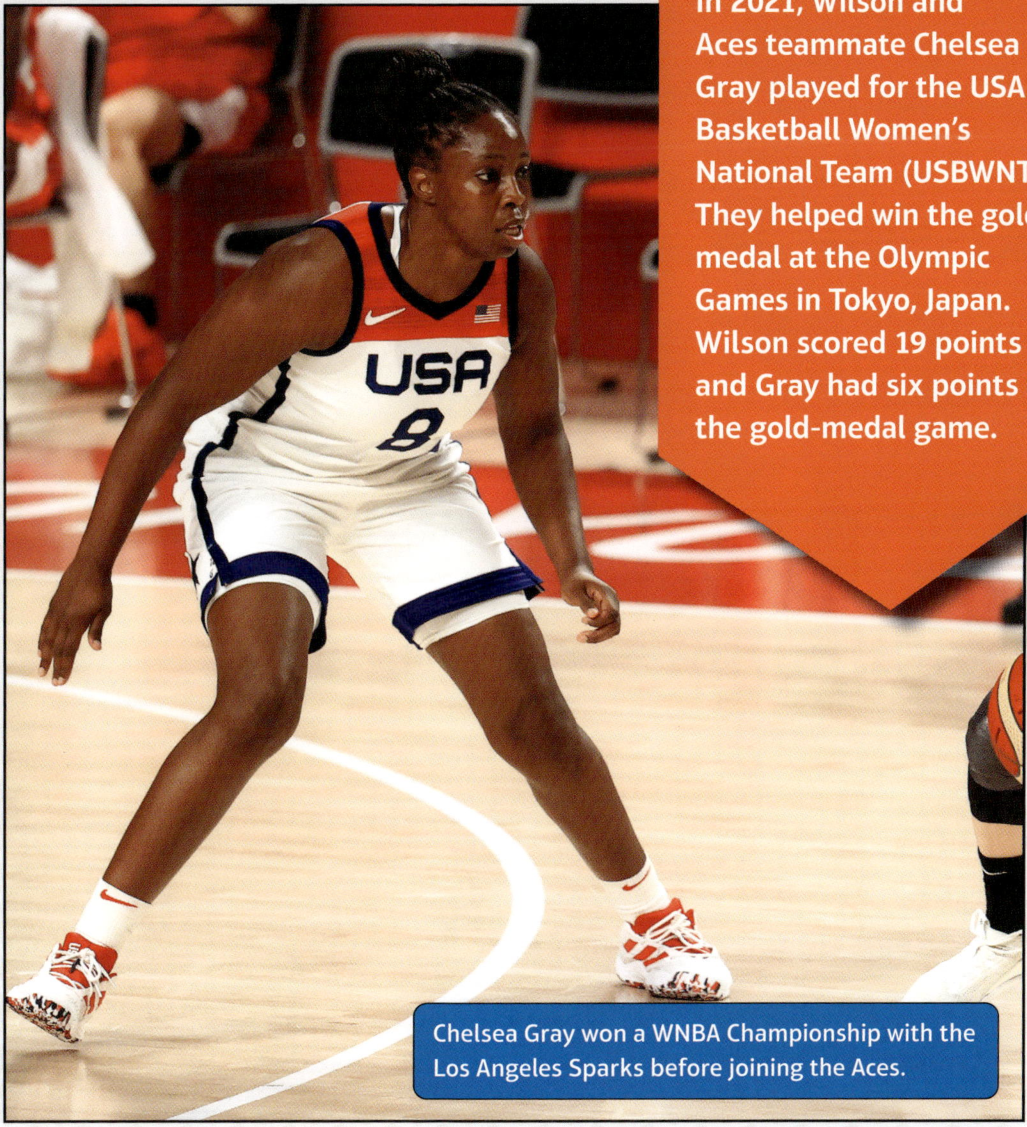

Chelsea Gray won a WNBA Championship with the Los Angeles Sparks before joining the Aces.

Hammon led the Stars in scoring and assists nearly every season she played. She decided to be a coach after retiring from playing in 2014. She spent eight seasons as an assistant coach with the San Antonio Spurs. In late 2021, the Aces hired Hammon to be their head coach.

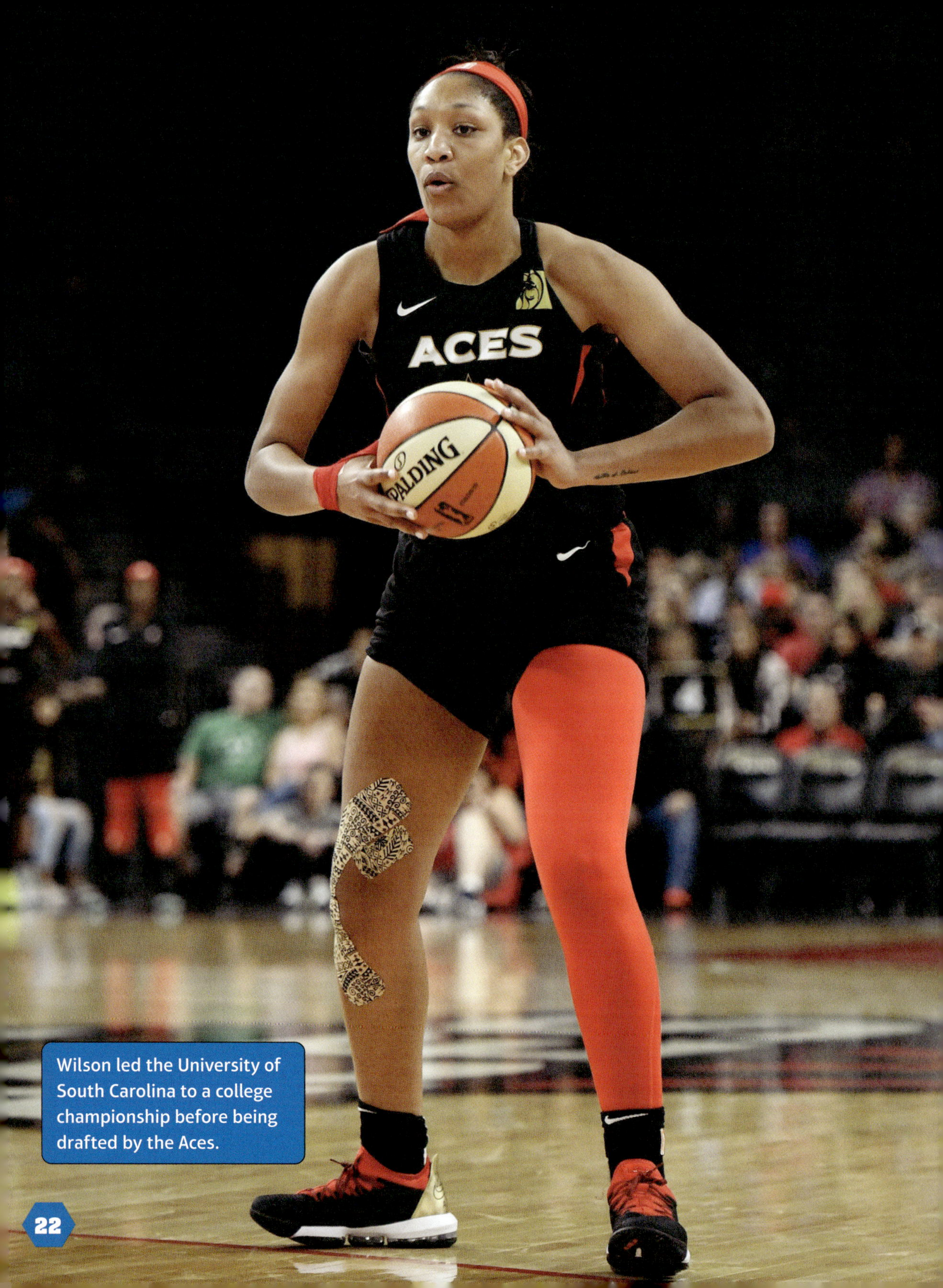

Wilson led the University of South Carolina to a college championship before being drafted by the Aces.

In 2018, Wilson was the number one overall draft pick and the Rookie of the Year. In each of her first four seasons with the Aces, she led the team in points per game. In three of those seasons, she also led in rebounds per game.

Wilson has played a huge role in her team's success. She led the Aces to three conference title games and one conference championship. The 6 feet, 4 inch (1.9 m) forward won the WNBA Most Valuable Player award in 2020. She has an exciting future with the Aces.

Wilson has been named to the WNBA All-Star team three of her four seasons with the Aces.

The Aces picked Kelsey Plum first overall in the 2017 WNBA Draft.

BREAKING BARRIERS

The Aces have many incredible players on their team. Five Aces players competed in the Tokyo Olympics in 2021. Chelsea Gray and Wilson won gold with the USBWNT. Aces center Ji-Su Park competed for South Korea's team.

Four Aces players, including Chelsea Gray (*left*) and A'ja Wilson (*right*), won Olympic gold as part of the USBWNT.

Aces guards Kelsey Plum and Jackie Young also competed for the US in the Tokyo Olympics. They played 3x3 basketball, a brand-new Olympic sport. In 3x3, each team has three players on the court and one backup. Plum, Young, and teammates Stefanie Dolson and Allisha Gray won the gold medal.

All the talent on the court has paid off for the Aces. The team is thrilling fans with amazing plays and big victories. Coach Hammon is ready to prove that she can lead a team of her own. With superstars like Wilson and Gray leading the way, a championship season is not far away.

Ji-Su Park was the second-youngest player to play in a WNBA game when she debuted for the Aces in 2018.

The Aces picked Jackie Young first overall in the WNBA Draft after she helped the University of Notre Dame win a college championship.

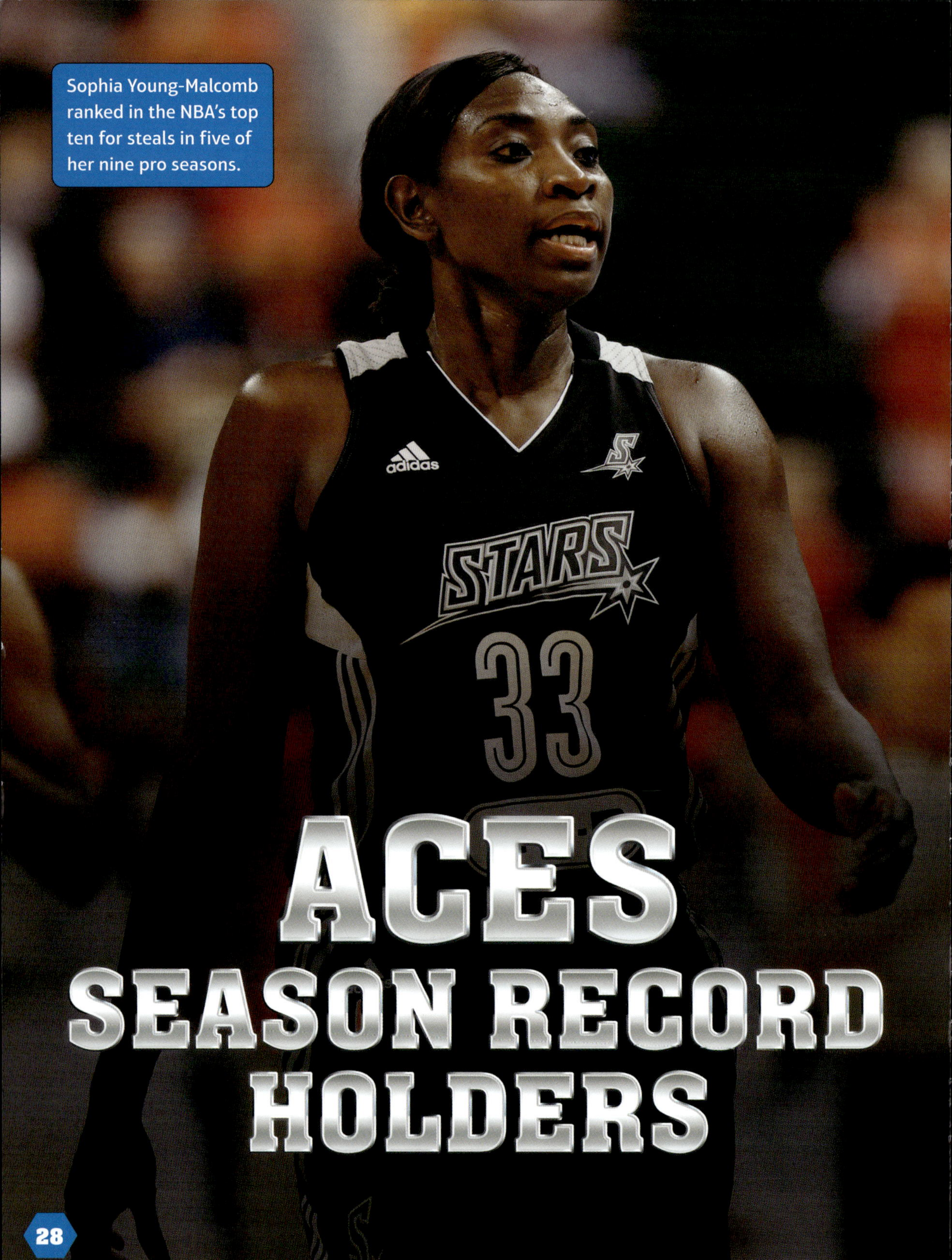

Sophia Young-Malcomb ranked in the NBA's top ten for steals in five of her nine pro seasons.

ACES SEASON RECORD HOLDERS

POINTS

1. A'ja Wilson, 682 (2018)
2. Becky Hammon, 604 (2009)
3. Sophia Young-Malcolm, 600 (2009)
4. A'ja Wilson, 584 (2021)
5. Becky Hammon, 582 (2008)

ASSISTS

1. Chelsea Gray, 202 (2019)
2. Becky Hammon, 192 (2011)
3. Chelsea Gray, 189 (2021)
4. Becky Hammon, 176 (2012)
5. Danielle Robinson, 174 (2014)

REBOUNDS

1. Natalie Williams, 336 (2000)
2. Natalie Williams, 308 (2001)
3. A'ja Wilson, 298 (2021)
4. Jayne Appel-Marinelli, 270 (2014)
5. A'ja Wilson, 264 (2018)

BLOCKED SHOTS

1. Margo Dydek, 114 (1998)
2. Margo Dydek, 113 (2001)
3. Margo Dydek, 107 (2002)
4. Margo Dydek, 100 (2003)
5. Margo Dydek, 96 (2000)

STEALS

1. Jia Perkins, 80 (2013)
2. Debbie Black, 77 (1999)
3. Sophia Young-Malcolm, 74 (2012)
4. Sophia Young-Malcolm, 67 (2011)
5. Shannon Johnson, 60 (2006)

THREE-POINT BASKETS

1. Becky Hammon, 80 (2012)
2. Becky Hammon, 77 (2008)
3. Becky Hammon, 76 (2009)
4. Becky Hammon, 75 (2011)
5. Becky Hammon, 74 (2007)

GLOSSARY

assist: a pass from a teammate that leads directly to a score

block: when a defender knocks away a shot before the ball reaches the hoop

center: a player who usually stays close to the basket and the middle of the court

conference: a group of teams that play against one another

draft: when teams take turns choosing new players

forward: a player who usually plays near the basket

guard: a player who plays in the backcourt in basketball

mascot: a person, animal, or object used as a symbol to stand for a sports team and to bring good luck

rebound: grabbing and controlling the ball after a missed shot

regular season: when all the teams in a league play one another to determine playoff teams

rookie: a first-year player

Semifinal: a game or a series of games coming before the final round in a tournament

LEARN MORE

Buckey, A. W. *Women in Basketball*. Lake Elmo, MN: Focus Readers, 2020.

Doeden, Matt. *G.O.A.T. Women's Basketball Teams*. Minneapolis: Lerner Publications, 2021.

Hill, Anne E. *A'ja Wilson*. Minneapolis: Lerner Publications, 2022.

Las Vegas Aces
https://aces.wnba.com/

WNBA
https://www.wnba.com/

Women's Basketball Hall of Fame
https://www.wbhof.com/

INDEX

PHOTO ACKNOWLEDGMENTS

Image credits: Julio Aguilar/Stringer/Getty Images, p.4; Julio Aguilar/Stringer/Getty Images, p.6; Julio Aguilar/Stringer/Getty Images, p.7; Otto Greule Jr/Stringer/Getty Images, p.8; Otto Greule Jr/Stringer/Getty Images, p.9; Christian Petersen/Staff/Getty Images, p.10; Domenic Centofanti/Stringer/Getty Images, p.11; Ethan Miller/Staff/Getty Images, p.12; Mike Ehrmann/Staff/Getty Images, p.13; Marcel Thomas/ZUMA Press/Newscom, p.14; Marcel Thomas/ZUMA Press/Newscom, p.15; Julio Aguilar/Stringer/Getty Images, p.16; Ethan Miller/Staff/Getty Images, p.17; Christian Petersen/Staff/Getty Images, p.18; Todd Warshaw/Staff/Getty Images, p.19; Greg Ashman/Cal Sport Media/Newscom, p.20; Mike Ehrmann/Staff/Getty Images, p.21; Ethan Miller/Staff/Getty Images, p.22; Ethan Miller/Staff/Getty Images, p.23; Christian Petersen/Staff/Getty Images, 24; Gregory Shamus/Staff/Getty Images, p.25; Ethan Miller/Staff/Getty Images, p.26; Ethan Miller/Staff/Getty Images, p.27; TMB/Icon SMI/Newscom, p.28

Design element: Master3D/Shutterstock.com.

Cover image: Ethan Miller/Staff/Getty Images